TINY BATTLEFIELDS

FIGHTING AIDS

MARY COLSON

Gareth Stevens
PUBLISHING

Please visit our website, www.garethstevens.com. For a free color catalog of all our high-quality books, call toll free 1-800-542-2595 or fax 1-877-542-2596.

Colson, Mary.
Fighting AIDS / by Mary Colson.
p. cm. -- (Tiny battlefields)
Includes index.
ISBN 978-1-4824-1356-4 (pbk.)
ISBN 978-1-4824-1306-9 (6-pack)
ISBN 978-1-4824-1452-3 (library binding)
1. AIDS (Disease) -- Juvenile literature. I. Colson, Mary. II. Title.
RC606.65 C65 2015
616.97--d23

Library of Congress Cataloging-in-Publication Data

First Edition

Published in 2015 by
Gareth Stevens Publishing
111 East 14th Street, Suite 349
New York, NY 10003

© 2015 Gareth Stevens Publishing

Produced by: Calcium, www.calciumcreative.co.uk
Designed by: Simon Borrough
Edited by: Sarah Eason and Jennifer Sanderson
Picture research by: Rachel Blount

Photo credits: Cover: Shutterstock: BioMedical; Inside: Centers for Disease Control and Prevention: James Gathany 45; Dreamstime: 1000words 22, Antonella865 12, Aprescindere 19, Viachaslau Bondarau 8, Matt Fowler 31, Jose Gil 17, Julesunlimited 14, Viacheslav Krisanov 10, Andrei Malov 13, Ferdinand Reus 20, Samrat35 16, Akbar Solo 41; Flickr: Afagen 11, NIAID 1, 9, 29; Medecins sans Frontieres: Andre Francois 25; Shutterstock: Alex011973 4, Alila Medical Media 32, BioMedical 6, Christian Darkin 3, 27, Katatonia82 35, Kvini 21, l i g h t p o e t 30, Dmitry Lobanov 23, Martynowi.cz 28, Lipowski Milan 34, Posztos 24, Dr. Morley Read 26, SNEHIT 15, Spectral-Design 42, Spirit of America 7, 20, 33, Spotmatik 40, Stocklight 39, Pal Teravagimov 5, 36, Vetpathologist 43; Wikimedia Commons: Todd Huffman 37, Gary van der Merwe 38, Luis Villa del Campo 44.

Printed in the United States of America

CPSIA compliance information: Batch #CS15GS: For further information contact Gareth Stevens, New York, New York at 1-800-542-2595.

Contents

CHAPTER 1: WAGING WAR

All over the world, a war is being waged against human health. From Africa to the United States and from Chile to China, in people's bodies millions of tiny cells are battling against a deadly virus that threatens to destroy entire communities. Doctors and scientists are locked in a race against the clock to create drugs to stop this disease in its tracks.

THE ENEMY ATTACKS: HIV AND AIDS

AIDS stands for acquired immunodeficiency syndrome. It is an infectious disease, which means it can be passed from one person to the next. Microorganisms called pathogens cause infectious diseases. There are three types of pathogens: virus, bacterium, and protozoon. The virus that causes AIDS is called the human immunodeficiency virus (HIV). HIV attacks the human immune system and eventually destroys it. It zooms in on white blood cells known as T cells. T cells are fighter cells that help the body fight off infections such as colds and chicken pox.

Ongoing laboratory research may provide improved treatments for HIV/AIDS in the future.

Nigeria has the highest HIV infection rate in the world.

HIV attaches itself to a T cell and then uses it to make many copies of itself. It is so deadly because it can copy itself amazingly quickly and takes over other T cells before they can destroy it. The T cells are then powerless to fight off infections of any kind, so the body's natural defenses are destroyed.

A GLOBAL FIGHT

It is estimated that there are 40 million people living with HIV or AIDS today. It is an epidemic that affects people from all walks of life.

"We now know that the number of people who will die of AIDS in the first decade of the twenty-first century will rival the number that died in all the wars in all the decades of the twentieth century."

Al Gore, former vice president of the United States

ENEMY VIRUS

HIV is a virus most commonly caught by having unprotected sex or by sharing infected needles and other injecting equipment used to take drugs.

WHEN THE VIRUS ATTACKS

The HIV virus attacks a person's immune system and weakens their ability to fight infections and disease. AIDS is the final stage of HIV infection, when the body can no longer fight life-threatening infections. Although there is currently no cure for HIV, treatment of the condition has improved greatly since the illness was first recognized. There are now a number of treatments that enable most people with the virus to live a long and healthy life.

FIGHTING BACK

Along with finding improved treatments for HIV/AIDS, doctors are now hopeful that a cure for HIV/AIDS will be possible. In recent years, a number of revolutionary studies, such as the "Mississippi baby" case, have shown that HIV can be eradicated in some patients.

The HIV virus attacks the body's immune system, making it impossible to fight even minor illnesses, such as colds and the flu.

On the Battlefield

In March 2013, a newborn that had become infected with HIV in its mother's uterus was treated aggressively with antiretroviral drugs. The treatment of the baby was a grueling daily task, and after 18 months of treatment, the mother decided to stop administering the drugs. Amazingly, when she did so, her daughter was still able to keep the virus in check, much to the surprise of physicians. The unusual case became known as the "Mississippi baby" case.

KNOWLEDGE IS POWER

The astounding results of the Mississippi baby case, and others like it, have encouraged scientists to believe that it may be possible to cure other babies and children infected with HIV by giving them an immediate and short-term course of antiretroviral drugs. The hope is that the patients' own immune systems will then ultimately fight and destroy the virus. Armed with this new knowledge, scientists are now trying to find a cure for all sufferers of HIV/AIDS. If they are successful, they will dramatically change the lives of millions of people worldwide.

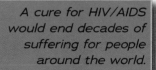
A cure for HIV/AIDS would end decades of suffering for people around the world.

7

Attacking the Body

The immune system protects the body against infection, but what makes up the immune system and how does it work? What happens when a virus such as HIV attacks?

The White Army

The immune system is a complex network of cells, tissues, and organs. It is also home to an amazing army of white blood cells. White blood cells are found all over the body, in the organs and even inside the bones in a thick, gooey gel called bone marrow. The body's white blood cells are the first line of defense against infection. White blood cells kill invading germs. They also remember germs so if, for example, a person catches a cold one year, the white blood cells will recognize those germs the next time that person catches a cold and know how to attack them. All these parts of the immune system combine their efforts to fight off infections and diseases. However, if a virus such as HIV attacks, the immune system itself is under threat.

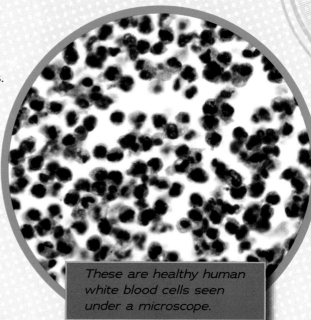

These are healthy human white blood cells seen under a microscope.

HIV Positive

A simple blood test can show if someone has traces of HIV in his or her body. If they do, they are called "HIV positive." If the virus is diagnosed early, there is a greater chance of the drugs working. With a combination of antiretroviral drugs, it is often possible for HIV positive people to continue to live with the virus, sometimes for many years, before developing AIDS.

On the Battlefield

One of the first symptoms displayed by a person with HIV is a flu-like illness. After that, HIV often causes no symptoms for several years, but continues to attack the immune system by copying itself and multiplying. Antiretroviral drugs are used to boost the body's white blood cell count to help fight the virus. Today, scientists are developing advanced antiretrovirals that target the virus itself and slow down its rate of reproduction.

This is a human cell that has been infected with HIV.

WHO IS AT RISK?

Before scientists knew how HIV was transmitted and how the virus behaved, many groups of people were at risk of becoming HIV positive. However, today, especially in many developed countries, people are taught how to keep themselves safe and HIV free.

FACTS AND FICTION

HIV is most commonly caught through unprotected sex, drug use by injecting with shared needles, and blood transfusions of infected blood. It is also passed to babies by their mothers during pregnancy and breast-feeding. There are lots of myths about how HIV can be caught, so it is important to separate the facts from the fiction. HIV lives in body fluids such as blood, semen, and breast milk. To contract HIV, one of these fluids from an infected person must get into another person's blood. Saliva, sweat, and urine do not contain enough of the virus to infect another person. HIV does not survive for long outside of the body, so it cannot be caught by using public swimming pools, sharing towels, holding hands, or kissing.

Many people catch HIV through injecting drugs using shared needles.

The AIDS quilt is an ever-growing memorial to over 90,000 people who have died of the disease in the United States.

THE RYAN WHITE STORY

Ryan White was born in 1971 with severe hemophilia, a disease that stops blood from clotting properly. Throughout his life, Ryan needed regular injections of blood and blood-clotting agents. When he was 13, he had a lung operation. During the operation, it was discovered that Ryan was HIV positive. At the time, not enough was known about the virus and how it was caught, and people were terrified that they would catch it, too. Ryan was banned from attending school. He and his parents began a long legal and media campaign to allow him to go to school, which they eventually won. Sadly, Ryan died of complications from AIDS in 1990.

"Because of the lack of education on AIDS, discrimination, fear, panic, and lies surrounded me ... We had great faith that with patience, understanding, and education, that my family and I could be helpful in changing their minds and attitudes around."

Ryan White

POSITIVE LEGACY

In the 1980s, thousands of hemophiliacs contracted HIV through blood transfusions. After Ryan White's death, the US government created the Ryan White Comprehensive AIDS Resources Emergency (CARE) Act. This is a fund to help people living with HIV/AIDS.

CHAPTER 2: A GLOBAL EPIDEMIC

Since HIV was discovered in the early 1980s, millions of people throughout the world have been infected with the virus. Most are adults, but some children are HIV positive, as are many babies. In many countries, public health programs educate people about safe sex and not sharing needles, and donated blood is screened for HIV. However, some developing countries are struggling to cope with extremely high HIV infection rates and millions of people living with AIDS.

HIV/AIDS is avoidable & preventable, Abstain or Practice Safe Sex

More than 10 percent of the Zambian population is HIV positive. The government runs publicity campaigns in an attempt to limit the spread of the virus.

VIRUS HISTORY

AIDS-related viruses have been around since the 1930s. Scientists have found a link between AIDS and a virus that affects the immune system of monkeys in Central Africa. It is not fully known how the virus transferred to humans. One theory is that, at some point, an infected animal bit a person. In 1959, the first known case of HIV in a human and the resulting death of that person was recorded in the area now known as the Democratic Republic of the Congo. Genetic studies of HIV suggest that the virus first arrived in the United States around 1966.

Understanding HIV/AIDS

Throughout the 1960s and 1970s, an unknown disease that caused numerous deaths baffled doctors around the world. Babies born to some prostitutes and drug users showed the same symptoms. Doctors were determined to know how this deadly virus behaved, how it was passed from person to person, and who was at risk of catching it. The virus seemed to be affecting three main groups—gay men, drug users who shared needles, and hemophiliacs and other patients who had had blood transfusions.

Naming the Virus

In 1986, French scientist Luc Montagnier named the virus "HIV." In the same year, a US scientist named Robert Gallo discovered that HIV was the virus that caused AIDS. The discoveries made by Montagnier and Gallo meant that researchers could start to develop drugs that might help win the war against HIV.

In the past, many thousands of people became HIV positive because they were given infected blood during operations.

AIDS AROUND THE WORLD

HIV/AIDS does not respect age, wealth, gender, or borders. It is a disease that affects people and communities all over the world. The worst affected areas are often places with low education and high poverty rates, but no one and no place is immune to the disease. The worst-affected countries are India and Nigeria, where the rapid rate of infection means that for every one person who receives treatment, four more people are infected with HIV.

HIV/AIDS affects people from all walks of life in every corner of the world.

CRISIS IN AFRICA

All of the top 20 countries most affected by HIV/AIDS are in Africa. Africa is home to about 15 percent of the world's population, but 69 percent of all people who live with HIV are found in Africa. South Africa has more than 6 million people living with HIV/AIDS. In Botswana, Malawi, Zimbabwe, Zambia, Mozambique, Namibia, and South Africa at least 10 percent of the population is HIV positive. More than 1 million new cases of HIV are now registered every year in Africa.

AIDS in Europe

Russia, Portugal, Ukraine, Estonia, and Latvia have the highest rates of HIV infection in Europe. More than 1.3 million people are HIV positive across these countries. Eastern Europe has the highest regional infection rate, with new HIV infections rising by 13 percent within the last 7 years. Western European infection rates seem to have peaked and are reasonably low as a result of the availability of antiretroviral drugs in those countries.

Rio de Janiero in Brazil has a high rate of HIV transmission.

Asia: An HIV Time Bomb?

Although officially more than 1 million HIV-positive people live in China, it is possible that the true, undisclosed number is much higher. Across Asia, there are high HIV positive numbers among certain groups such as injecting drug users and prostitutes.

AIDS in the Americas

In the United States, there are approximately 1 million HIV-positive people, with this number slowly increasing every year. However, with better medicines, education programs, and early diagnosis, the death rates from AIDS are decreasing. Unfortunately, in Central and South America, HIV rates are increasing every year, particularly in large cities such as Mexico City and Rio de Janiero.

"Three decades into this crisis, let us set our sights on achieving the "three zeros"— zero new HIV infections, zero discrimination, and zero AIDS-related deaths."

Ban Ki-moon,
UN secretary-general

LIVING WITH AIDS

Millions of people all over the world face living with HIV/AIDS every day. Drugs, therapies, and care are usually available in developed countries, and there are laws protecting people against discrimination in their jobs. However, in the developing world, things are very different. Wherever people live, living with HIV/AIDS can be challenging, difficult, and emotional.

There are more than 6 million men, women, and children in India living with HIV/AIDS.

TREATING THE YOUNG

The World Health Organization (WHO) estimates that around the world 2.3 million children are HIV positive and there are more than 300,000 new infections each year. However, not all infected children are receiving treatment. Around 250,000 children die each year because they have not received drugs. Without the right medication, 50 percent of HIV-infected children will die before the age of two. In order to tackle this problem, WHO is working with governments, medical charities, and health professionals to ensure that all children have access to HIV treatment by 2025. If this plan works, it will prevent an estimated 10 million AIDS-related deaths.

HIV Teens

Between 2005 and 2013, there was a 50 percent increase in AIDS-related deaths in the 10-to-19 age group worldwide. This is a huge challenge for science and health care communities. Researchers in sociology, psychology, and medicine are now working together to create teen-friendly tests to encourage teenagers to be tested and to know their HIV status. In many countries, being HIV positive carries a huge stigma, and people fear being cast out or shunned. Counseling services are being improved to help teenagers cope with their HIV status and to encourage them to keep taking their antiretroviral drugs.

"HIV/AIDS is a disease with a stigma. And we have learned with experience, not just with HIV/AIDS, but with other diseases, countries for many reasons are sometimes hesitant to admit they have a problem."

Margaret Chan, WHO director general

The cost of providing adequate care for HIV/AIDS patients is high. Here, people are protesting against cuts to HIV/AIDS services in California.

ATTACKING AIDS AND GETTING TREATMENT

Around the world, more than 7 million HIV-positive people have no access to medical treatment. The vast majority of these people live in Africa in countries such as South Africa, Botswana, and Swaziland.

On the Battlefield

Before 2005, the South African government did not prioritize HIV. Infection rates were skyrocketing and only a handful of those with HIV received treatment. With increased government support came a new attitude and a desire to attack the crisis. Today, the country has the world's biggest program of HIV/AIDS drug treatment. Nearly 2 million people now receive antiretroviral drugs each day in South Africa. Life expectancy for people with HIV has risen from 54 to 60 in just a few years, and AIDS-related deaths are falling. However, with nearly a 1,000 people becoming HIV positive every day, there is an enormous battle still to be won.

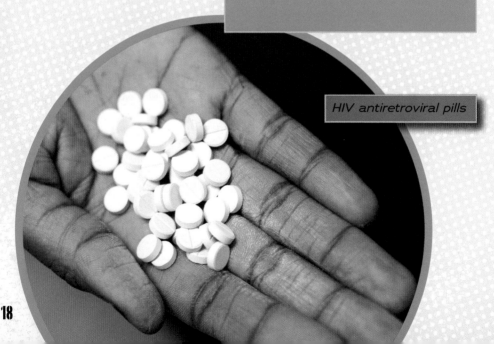

HIV antiretroviral pills

The Front Line

Caring for people with HIV/AIDS and ensuring they receive the right treatment is very challenging in a country with a high rural population. In South African cities, AIDS clinics are like medical facilities in any developed country—modern, clean, and efficient. However, with a large rural population spread over a vast landscape, the challenge for doctors and nurses can be simply getting to patients. Old mobile homes, trailers, tents, even suitcases in car trunks are all used at times to get the medicine to those who need it. There are few roads into the African bushlands, and at some times of year, the rains flood the rough tracks, making it more difficult to travel.

New Drugs Mean New Hope

In 2013, the South African government announced a new treatment program for HIV patients. Instead of three antiretroviral pills twice a day, patients will take just one new antiretroviral pill once a day. The cost of treating each patient has gone down, too, so it is hoped that even more people will be able to receive treatment for the virus. The new pill is also particularly effective at stopping HIV-positive pregnant or breast-feeding women from passing the virus on to their babies and children.

Women are particularly vulnerable to the spread of HIV/AIDS for cultural reasons. The virus can be passed on to unborn children in the uterus.

CHAPTER 3: THE IMPACT OF AIDS

HIV/AIDS does not just affect human health, it can affect a country's economy, too. If enough people are too sick to work, there will be many jobs that go undone. This has an impact on a country's ability to develop and prosper, so it falls even farther behind the rest of the world. The side effects of HIV can be almost as devastating as the virus itself. What large- and small-scale medical and scientific programs are in place to help and to deal with this issue?

COUNTERING AN AFRICAN EPIDEMIC

Across Africa, thousands of doctors, teachers, farmers, parents, politicians, lawyers, and children are dying from AIDS. In developed countries with high education rates and well-established social and health infrastructures, the impact is not felt as keenly, but in developing countries, such as Botswana, Zimbabwe, and Zambia, the impact is crippling. The Centers for Disease Control and Prevention (CDC) helps countries to build their health care capacities, including counseling for HIV victims and providing vital medicine to pregnant women to stop them passing on HIV to their babies.

Education is vital to help developing countries lower the HIV/AIDS rate in Africa.

Many poor communities across the world rely on aid agencies for food as well as HIV medicine.

BOTSWANA AT BREAKING POINT?

The small southern African country of Botswana has a total population of only 2 million. It is one of the most sparsely populated countries on Earth, but more than one-quarter of its adult population is HIV positive. Between 1999 and 2005, the country lost 17 percent of its health-care workforce to AIDS. In 1996, the Botswana-Harvard Partnership was established. This led to a new laboratory being opened in Gabarone, the capital city, in 2001. There, professors and researchers from Harvard work alongside Botswanan scientists to study the virus and to train health-care workers.

On the Battlefield

UNAIDS is the Joint United Nations Program on HIV/AIDS. It was set up in 1996 to coordinate the global fight against HIV transmission. It campaigns for awareness, raises funds, and helps governments organize a response to HIV and tackle the virus in their own countries. UNAIDS estimates that one in six people in Botswana has HIV. This makes it the second highest infection rate in the world after the country of Swaziland. The Botswanan government has focused much of the money and medicine on pregnant women who are HIV positive. This has successfully lowered the number of virus transmissions from mother to child from 40 percent to just 4 percent.

AIDS AND POVERTY

If one person in a household becomes HIV positive, the impact is significant. It might become difficult for that person to work, so the household income may go down. People might stop talking to the person out of fear or ignorance. At worst, he or she may even be shunned or forced to leave the community, and this could lead to poverty.

In some parts of the world, being HIV positive can lead to poverty and homelessness.

AFFECTING THE FAMILY

AIDS and poverty are often linked in a devastating downward spiral. For example, if an already poor rural Indian farmer becomes HIV positive, he may not be able to grow food for his family, leaving them with an uncertain food supply. It could also mean he is unable to earn money, so either his wife has to find work or the whole family falls into even worse poverty. If thousands or millions of people are in this position, the country's economy will be affected. The country will be less wealthy and not have money for drugs, schools, or development.

A new HIV test uses dried blood spots. If the virus is detected early, the treatment is more effective.

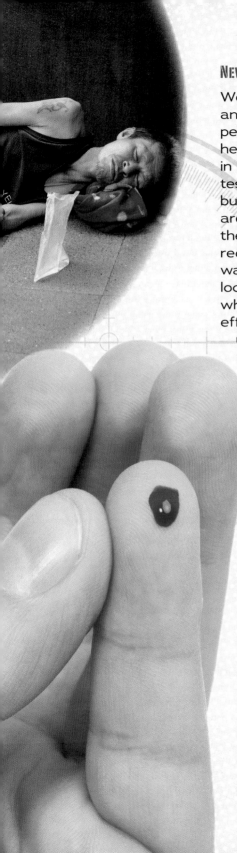

New Tests, New Drugs

We know that if HIV is diagnosed early and appropriate treatment is taken, people can lead long and essentially healthy lives. Up until now, people in rural areas have struggled to be tested and to gain access to drugs, but new tests and new drug programs are now making a real difference to these people. Previously, an HIV test required a liquid blood sample. If this was taken from a patient in a rural location, it had to be refrigerated, which may not have been practical or effective. Now, however, a new test using dried blood spots has been invented. This procedure is called biosampling. The blood samples are blotted and dried on filter paper. They can then be very easily sent without refrigeration to a laboratory for testing. With a quicker test and targeted treatment, being HIV positive does not mean that countries with high infection rates need suffer even more.

"We live in an . . . interdependent world, which simply means we cannot escape each other. How we respond to AIDS depends, in part, on whether we understand this interdependence. It is not someone else's problem. This is everybody's problem."

Bill Clinton, former US president

MONEY AND MEDICINE

People with HIV need drugs that can be expensive to buy. The price of HIV antiretroviral medicines has become cheaper over time, but the newest, most effective drugs are so expensive that only wealthy nations and people with health insurance can afford them. UNAIDS and Doctors Without Borders organizations such as Médecins Sans Frontières (MSF) are campaigning to change this.

COUNTING THE COST

When a pharmaceutical company develops a drug, it will spend many millions of dollars on research and testing. The company is a business, so it must regain the cost of research through the price of the new drug. This is why new medicines, particularly for HIV treatment, are so expensive. The company will patent the new drug, which means that only the company is allowed to produce the drug for a certain length of time.

HIV/AIDS drugs have become cheaper but are still out of reach for people in most developing countries.

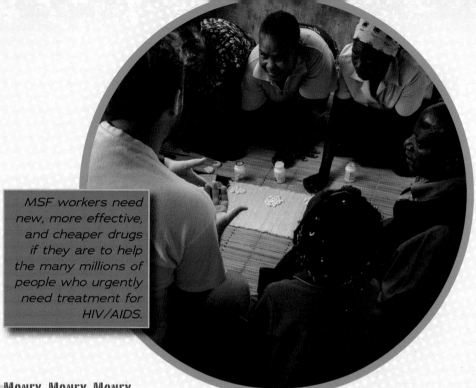

MSF workers need new, more effective, and cheaper drugs if they are to help the many millions of people who urgently need treatment for HIV/AIDS.

Money, Money, Money

HIV drugs are expensive and, in the developing world, $300 per person is too much for most countries to afford. In 2005, the Clinton Foundation negotiated a deal with drug companies to halve the cost for 122 nations around the world. This helped to ensure more HIV-positive people got the medicine they needed. Today, some drug companies are participating in the Medicines Patent Pool. This is an agreement in which a pharmaceutical company allows another company to make cheaper copies of its AIDS drugs. The best AIDS drugs are three or four medicines combined in one pill so taking the drug is easy and manageable for the patient. If more companies join the Medicines Patent Pool, the future cost of the medicine could fall even lower.

"It's good news that the price of key HIV drugs continues to fall ..., but the newer medicines are still priced far too high. MSF and other care providers need the newer treatments for people that have exhausted all other options, but patents keep them priced beyond reach."

Dr. Jennifer Cohn, medical director at MSF's Access Campaign

CHAPTER 4: SCIENCE FIGHTS BACK

Ever since HIV was officially identified in the 1980s, scientists have been locked in a battle to beat it. What exactly are scientists and researchers doing to fight the disease, is there any hope of finding a cure, and where might it be found?

GLOBAL BATTLE

If a cure for HIV/AIDS were found, the lives of millions all over the world would be drastically changed. Today, HIV research is often a global partnership with scientists from different countries and disciplines working together. Many medicines come from plants, especially those in rain forests, so plant biologists work alongside human biologists and biochemists. Much of the latest research, however, is focused on a cure possibly being found within the immune system itself.

An HIV/AIDS cure could be found in a rain forest plant.

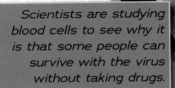

Scientists are studying blood cells to see why it is that some people can survive with the virus without taking drugs.

On the Battlefield

Research scientists are currently looking into why it is that some HIV positive people seem to be able to control the virus without drugs, and they think they may have found the answer. HIV copies or replicates itself, so it can mount a huge attack on a person's immune system. Some people have an extra protein in their blood that stops this copying process. The protein is called APOBEC3G (A3 for short) and it seems that some people have a naturally higher amount of A3 in their blood cells. A treatment that preserved high levels of A3 might mean that many more people would be able to control HIV without medication.

THE BERLIN PATIENT

In Berlin in 2009, an HIV-positive man named Timothy Ray Brown received a bone marrow transplant to treat leukemia. The bone marrow donor was naturally immune to HIV, and it seemed as if the immunity was passed on to Timothy Brown. After the transplant, Timothy no longer needed antiretroviral drugs to control HIV. Other doctors in the United States and France have since reported similar cases. Scientists estimate that about 10 percent of people might be naturally immune to HIV. Biologists believe that those people create antibodies that bind to a protein called gp120 on the outside of the virus cell. Gp120 helps the virus find a host cell in the body, but the antibodies seem to stop this process.

MICROBIOLOGICAL BATTLEFIELDS

Microbiology is the study of tiny organisms such as viruses. Viruses are minute— the size of only 10 to 800 nanometers, which is so small that they can be seen only through a special electron microscope. Microbiologists studying HIV are looking for its weak spots—the chinks in its armor. It is a long and painstaking process of study, research, testing, and reviewing.

Virus Variations

Almost all viruses mutate. This means that they change over time. There are at least two main HIV viruses in the world that microbiologists are studying. HIV-1 and HIV-2 are transmitted in the same ways, but HIV-2 is a strain of HIV usually found only in West Africa. It seems that a person who becomes infected with HIV-2 will remain well for a longer period before becoming sick than someone with HIV-1. Microbiologists do not yet know why this happens.

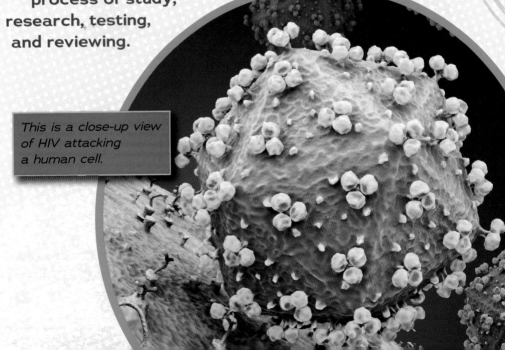

This is a close-up view of HIV attacking a human cell.

Doctors now treat each HIV/AIDS sufferer independently depending on the results of their initial tests.

On the Battlefield

An HIV test usually involves a patient giving a blood or urine sample. The doctors look at the sample for evidence of antibodies. The immune system produces antibodies when it recognizes an intruder, such as bacteria or a virus. The antibodies multiply to try to fight off the infection. Doctors test for a patient's "viral load." A positive HIV test means that a person's viral load is high. Doctors also monitor a patient's white blood cell or T cell count. If the count is low, a patient is more at risk of becoming sick so drugs are given to boost it. At the same time, other antiretroviral drugs target the viral load and work to reduce it.

VIRUS EXPOSURE

Scientists have now created medicines that can stop a person becoming HIV positive, even if they have been exposed to the virus. Anti-HIV medication is called PEP, which stands for post-exposure prophylaxis. If the PEP is begun within three days of exposure to HIV, there is a chance the person will not become infected.

TESTING VACCINES

Most people in developed countries have had injections to protect them from various illnesses such as measles and polio. Is it possible to make people immune to HIV? Is a vaccine really possible, and how are new drugs tested?

HIV/AIDS drugs can be tested on monkeys because they have similar immune systems to humans.

On the Battlefield

Vaccines work by making a person's immune system produce more antibodies to fight disease without actually infecting the person with it. If people come into contact with the disease at a later date, their system will recognize it and produce the antibodies needed to fight it off. In 2013, Brazilian scientists developed an HIV vaccine that they are currently testing on monkeys. Monkeys have similar immune systems to humans, and they also suffer from a virus similar to HIV. The vaccine is called HIVBr18, and scientists are hopeful that it could be a real breakthrough in the fight against HIV/AIDS. The current HIVBr18 vaccine will not kill off the virus, but it could keep it under control so that the infected person will not develop AIDS or pass on the virus to someone else.

Science versus the Virus

It is difficult to make a vaccine for HIV because the virus changes so quickly—it is always at least one step ahead of the drugs. HIV is such a super-virus that it can attack by hiding inside a person's immune cells—the immune system does not even know there is an intruder inside.

Some people have generated their own natural, genetic immunity against HIV. Scientists are looking at the immune systems of these people to figure out how they work, in the hope that they will be able to copy the systems and so help other HIV-infected people.

A Question of Time

Finding an affordable cure for HIV/AIDS that can be easily distributed around the world is still some way off. Even if a vaccine or potential breakthrough were to happen, years of trials, first on animals and then on humans, would be needed before the treatment was approved for use among the HIV-positive population.

Getting medical care to people in remote places is a challenge. Often clinics are in small houses built by the community.

TARGETING THE VIRUS

Many medicines have side effects and HIV drugs are no different. Side effects are symptoms that are not to do with the infection, but with the body's reaction to a drug. This might include sickness, headaches, or far more serious conditions such as organ failure. This means that other drugs need to be taken to control the side effects, which results in the patient having to take even more medicine. Scientists are now looking at alternatives to powerful drugs, and they are taking the battle right to the heart of the human immune system—and the virus itself.

"We have a very small group of patients called elite controllers, who have never received treatment—but their infection and the replication of the virus is controlled naturally ... We need to better understand the mechanism in their cells."

Professor Françoise Barre-Sinoussi, Nobel Prize-winning virologist

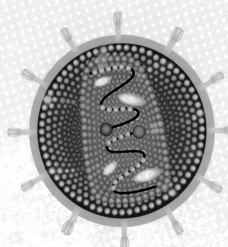

Scientists know the structure of HIV and are figuring out ways to attack it.

Uncloaking HIV

Scientists are learning more and more about HIV all the time. They now know that it is surrounded by a shield or cloak of molecules, which makes the virus invisible to the immune system. Making drugs that target the cloak is the next stage. If the virus cannot hide, the immune system will know it is there and will start responding immediately. This will stop the virus from replicating itself.

Treatment Resistance

Eventually, all HIV antiretroviral treatment stops working because the virus mutates and develops a resistance to the medicine. This is when HIV develops into AIDS. It may take many years or even a whole lifetime to happen, but it will occur. When it does, the patient's immune system is dangerously low and that leaves them vulnerable to other infections. Even a common cold can leave an AIDS patient extremely sick, with many medical complications such as lung problems and organ failure. However, doctors now know that if a patient begins treatment soon after infection, it will take longer for the virus to become resistant to the medicine. This means that the patient will be healthy for a longer time.

Some HIV patients such as this Kenyan woman are not treated early enough and AIDS develops. This can shorten their lives dramatically.

CHAPTER 5: EDUCATING THE WORLD

HIV/AIDS is one of the greatest threats to a country's security and development. Educating people about HIV and teaching them how to protect themselves is a key priority for many governments. Charities work alongside health and development agencies around the world to deliver AIDS education programs.

DIFFICULT WORK

AIDS education is challenging and sensitive work because it is not just about informing people—it often involves trying to change negative attitudes and long-held cultural beliefs about the disease. On a positive note, celebrity campaigners raise awareness of the disease and help to raise millions of dollars for HIV research.

It's Never too Early to Get Tested for HIV

Free HIV Testing & Treatment

TEST& treat

www.testandtreat.org

This poster in Mombasa, Kenya, is funded by an American health care foundation. Stopping the spread of HIV is in everybody's interest.

CULTURAL BATTLE

Desmond Tutu is a South African archbishop emeritus who has long campaigned for greater understanding of HIV. He works to end the stigma of being HIV positive within South African culture. For example, many people are thrown out of their communities for becoming HIV positive. The doctors, nurses, health workers, and counselors at the Desmond Tutu HIV Foundation deliver outreach education programs. They go to the villages and remote townships in rural South Africa to explain HIV, how it is caught, and what can be done to prevent it.

CHANGING ATTITUDES

AIDS educators around the world challenge cultural attitudes toward the disease and try to change risky social and sexual behaviors to keep people safe. For example, many men refuse to use condoms for religious or cultural reasons, and this is one of the key battles in changing attitudes, keeping people safe, and limiting infections. People who have multiple sexual partners and do not practice safe sex also put themselves at a higher risk of becoming infected. The problem is that changing attitudes and persuading people to live differently takes time, and all the while the virus is spreading.

Charity concerts raise a great deal of money for HIV/AIDS research and raise awareness about what it is like to live with HIV/AIDS.

"People with HIV are still stigmatized. The infection rates are going up. People are dying. The political response is appalling. The sadness of it, the waste."

Elton John,
Elton John AIDS Foundation

KNOWLEDGE IS POWER

It is fewer than 30 years since the first HIV cases were diagnosed, and in that time, HIV education has had a real impact in some parts of the world. The most successful education programs have targeted specific groups of vulnerable people such as young men, sex industry workers, drug users, and women.

FEMALE FOCUS

In many cultures, women and men are not treated equally, and this can make women much more vulnerable to HIV infection. Poorer women are not always educated so they do not know how to keep themselves safe. Lack of education may limit the work they can find, and they may be forced to work in the sex industry to earn money. The UN and many charities are focusing on female education as a way of keeping families and communities together and minimizing the number of AIDS orphans.

Nearly 10 percent of Swaziland's total population are orphans due to HIV/AIDS.

On the Battlefield

Just a few years ago, Uganda had a high HIV infection rate. Today, that number is much lower thanks to an education program created by the government, charities, and other organizations such as faith groups and women's groups. The highly successful program focuses on changing high-risk sexual behavior, such as not using condoms, along with religious beliefs. AIDS patients have been involved, and they too have spoken to people to create greater understanding. People in Uganda are now more aware of who is vulnerable, what HIV/AIDS means in terms of illness, and how they can remain safe through being faithful to one partner and making healthy lifestyle choices.

NEEDLE EXCHANGES

The CDC estimates that one in five of all new HIV infections is caused by sharing needles when injecting drugs. In the United States, the United Kingdom, Australia, and many other countries, needle exchanges are helping to limit the spread of HIV as well as other serious diseases such as hepatitis C. The needle exchange may be health workers handing out clean needles and syringes on the street or a clinic where drug users can go to get free, clean needles.

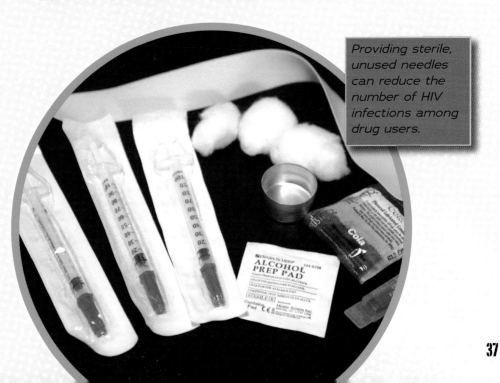

Providing sterile, unused needles can reduce the number of HIV infections among drug users.

CELEBRITY, CHARITY, AND CAMPAIGNING

At the Academy Awards ceremony, the American Music Awards, the San Francisco marathon, and every day on the street, you will see people wearing a red AIDS ribbon. The "crossed-over" ribbon has been an international symbol of support for people with HIV/AIDS since the early 1990s. The money raised from the sales of red ribbons goes to HIV/AIDS research. Who raises money, how do charities use the money, and what can people do to help in the fight against HIV/AIDS?

STAR ATTRACTION

UNAIDS and WHO believe that HIV infection rates have largely peaked in the developed world, so HIV/AIDS is no longer at the forefront of people's minds. Now that AIDS is mainly a problem only in Africa, the Caribbean, India, and South

The red ribbon symbolizes support for people living with HIV/AIDS.

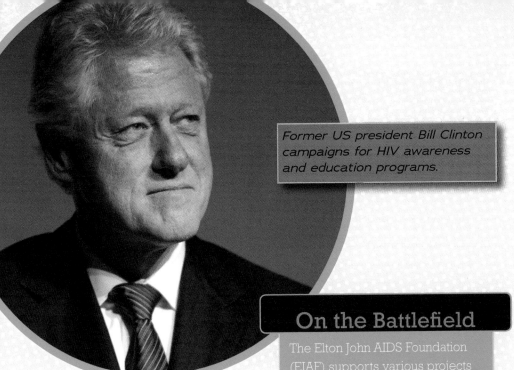

Former US president Bill Clinton campaigns for HIV awareness and education programs.

America, it is no longer a visible problem for many people, and it is easy to forget about the scale of the epidemic. The singers Bono and Sir Elton John both campaign for their HIV/AIDS foundations. They use their celebrity to attract millions of dollars of donations for HIV research, education programs, drugs, and raising awareness. Former politicians such as Bill Clinton and the late Nelson Mandela have also campaigned for HIV awareness and helped to bring the reality of the epidemic to the attention of people in the West.

On the Battlefield

The Elton John AIDS Foundation (EJAF) supports various projects in the Caribbean. After Africa, the Caribbean is the second-most affected region in the world in terms of HIV rates, but is often overlooked because of the scale of the problem elsewhere. More than 2 percent of the population of the Bahamas, Belize, Guyana, Haiti, and Trinidad and Tobago is HIV positive. AIDS is the leading cause of death in adults between 15 and 44 years old. There are low literacy rates and high poverty rates in the Caribbean. There is also a huge social stigma surrounding HIV so many infected people become homeless. EJAF funds care programs, counseling services, shelters, and education programs through which patients can access support.

CHAPTER 6: FUTURE HOPES AND CHALLENGES

With growing HIV infection rates in the developing world, what does the future hold in the battle against HIV/AIDS? How will scientists next try to attack the virus? Is a cure a realistic hope?

On the Battlefield

Many researchers around the globe are prioritizing the development of an effective HIV vaccine. With clinical trials set to start taking place on humans, it is hoped that a vaccine may be possible within 10 years. However, this may be too optimistic. Clinical trials of new drugs can take many years to be carried out. For example, in 2003, a trial in Thailand of an experimental vaccine known as RV144 showed that it was 31 percent effective in preventing HIV infection. More than 16,000 volunteers aged 18 to 30 took part in the trial. The volunteers were tested for HIV every six months, and the trial finished in 2006. The results were assessed and finally published in 2009. Since 2009, the researchers have continued to develop the vaccine. It will have to be retrialed and the results reassessed.

Developing new drugs takes many years of painstaking research, testing, and reviewing.

A Cautionary Tale

One of the biggest challenges facing researchers and campaigners in developed countries is keeping HIV/AIDS in the public eye. Most of the news about HIV is about the high infection rates in Africa and, as a result, HIV elsewhere can become overlooked. While infection numbers have largely stabilized in the West, HIV/AIDS is still classed as an epidemic, and public awareness and education need to remain a top priority. Knowledge of how the virus can be caught needs to be combined with safe lifestyle choices if the infection rates are to remain stable.

Raising Awareness

Every year, December 1 is World AIDS Day. The first World AIDS Day took place in 1988. Special events such as pop concerts, memorials, art projects, and fundraisers take place all over the world. The day is a reminder that there is a long way to go to beat the virus and that people living with HIV still suffer from stigma, discrimination, and enormous prejudice.

Raising awareness of HIV and how it can be transmitted is key to stopping its spread. Here, an HIV-positive campaigner takes part in a World AIDS Day event in Indonesia.

WHAT BATTLES REMAIN?

With all scientific progress, there are obstacles and barriers to success. It might be a lack of money, a lack of will, or a cultural attitude. The fight against HIV/AIDS has experienced all of these at different times in its history. When the virus was first discovered in the 1980s, the scientific world responded with urgency and energy. As the years have gone on and more than 25 million lives have been lost, the response has changed. Now, scientists are focusing their time and energies on the tiniest battlefield of all—the virus itself.

WORKING TOGETHER

Widespread scientific collaboration is the way forward for HIV research. A team of British and US scientists is working on a type of drug that will target each individual's HIV symptoms. A US-French-Australian team is looking at why a small amount of HIV remains even after treatment. Other scientists are investigating new "smart drugs" that can zoom in on infected cells. Stem cell research is also taking place, with the hope that it may provide some more medical weapons against HIV. All scientists share their research findings at conferences and in academic journals, which are also published online.

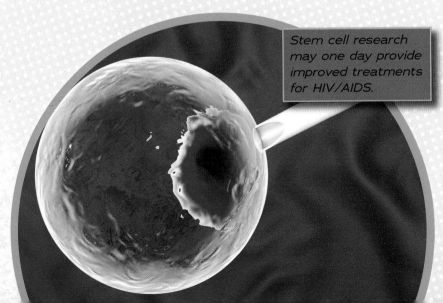

Stem cell research may one day provide improved treatments for HIV/AIDS.

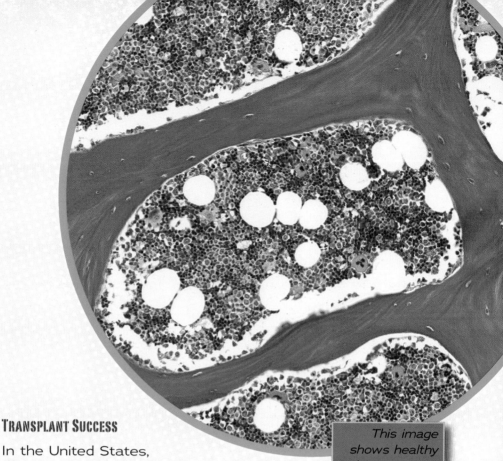

This image shows healthy bone marrow as seen under a microscope.

TRANSPLANT SUCCESS

In the United States, doctors have reported that two HIV-positive men seemed to become HIV clear after bone marrow transplants. Both patients have stopped taking HIV medicine and are now described as being "functionally cured" of HIV. This means that their bodies seem to be healthy and virus-free. The doctors do not yet fully understand how this has happened, but it is yet another hopeful development in the fight against HIV.

On the Battlefield

Scientists are making breakthroughs all the time in the battle against HIV. Danish researchers are testing a process that brings HIV out of its hiding places and to the surface of cells. The immune system can then destroy it. If the trials are successful, HIV could be as treatable as tonsillitis.

CAN THE WAR BE WON?

Is an HIV-free future possible? How will the virus change next? Will science and human effort beat HIV and win the war against the disease?

A BRIGHT FUTURE?

Today, with advanced retroviral treatment, people with HIV can lead full and normal lives. By 2015, it is estimated that more than half of people living with HIV will be 50 years old or older. However, as people have discovered, the global battle against HIV is one that is still being fought.

AIDS memorials are a tragic reminder of the many lives lost.

All over the world, people remain vulnerable to becoming infected with the disease because of low education, cultural or religious beliefs, unsafe sex, sharing needles when injecting drugs, or infected blood transfusions. There are major HIV awareness campaigns in many countries, and a huge amount of government money and charity fundraising provides the funds for vital scientific research.

"AIDS today in Africa is claiming more lives than the sum total of all wars, famines and floods, and the ravages of such deadly diseases as malaria ... We must act now for the sake of the world."

Nelson Mandela,
former South African president

Amazing progress has already been made in the fight against HIV/AIDS, but more research is needed if the war against the disease is to be finally won.

A WAR ON ALL FRONTS

HIV/AIDS treatments are developing all the time, and for many people, the disease is no longer the death sentence it once was. There are nearly 30 approved HIV/AIDS drugs in use around the world that treat different stages of the virus's progress. HIV may remain one step ahead of science for a while longer, but the will to find a cure is strong. New battlegrounds are opening up all the time as science attacks the virus on all fronts. It might be a tiny battlefield taking place on a microscopic level, but the war against HIV/AIDS is enormous.

GLOSSARY

ANTIBODIES the proteins that fight infections

ANTIRETROVIRALS drugs that control viruses

CLINICAL TRIAL the testing of a medicine with a small group of animals or humans

DISCRIMINATION unfair treatment because of prejudice

ELECTRON MICROSCOPE a powerful microscope that uses beams of electrons to create a greatly magnified image

EPIDEMIC a fast-spreading disease

GENETIC STUDIES looking at the DNA of cells

HEPATITIS C a very serious liver disease that can be fatal

INFRASTRUCTURES large-scale systems

MUTATE to change, or evolve

MOLECULE the smallest part of a chemical compound

NANOMETERS billionths of a meter

OPTIMISTIC extremely positive

ORGANS body parts with a specific function

OUTREACH PROGRAMS programs in which people go out into communities to actively engage with or educate the people

PATENT to secure the exclusive rights to an invention

PROTEIN a part of the structure of all living cells and viruses

STIGMA shame or disgrace attached to someone by society

TISSUES nerves and muscles

VACCINES weakened versions of a disease that is given to people to protect them from the full-blown version

VIRAL LOAD the amount of HIV in a person's blood

VIRUS a disease caused by a particle that replicates itself

VIRUS TRANSMISSION the way in which a virus is passed from one person to another

For More Information

Books

Chilman-Blair, Kim. *Medikidz Explain HIV* (Superheroes on a Medical Mission). New York, NY: Rosen Central, 2010.

Dicker, Katie. *AIDS & HIV* (Global Issues). New York, NY: Rosen Central, 2011.

Lew, Kristi. *How Scientists Research Cells* (Cells: The Building Blocks of Life). New York, NY: Chelsea House Publishing, 2011.

Yount, Lisa. *Luc Montagnier: Identifying the AIDS Virus* (Trailblazers in Science and Technology). New York, NY: Chelsea House Publishing, 2011.

Websites

Explore the human body and find out more about cells at:
www.kidsbiology.com/human_biology/

Check out the website of the UN Children's Organization, UNICEF, to find out more about HIV, AIDS orphans, and what the UN is doing to fight the epidemic at:
www.unicef.org/aids

Find out what is happening near you or what you can do to take part in World AIDS Day at:
www.worldaidsday.org

Publisher's note to educators and parents: Our editors have carefully reviewed these websites to ensure that they are suitable for students. Many websites change frequently, however, and we cannot guarantee that a site's future contents will continue to meet our high standards of quality and educational value. Be advised that students should be closely supervised whenever they access the Internet.

INDEX